Gluten Free:

Gluten Free Slow Cooker Recipes

Simple, Quick And Delicious Gluten Free Slow Cooker Recipes For Beginners

Table of Contents

Introduction

This book contains 40 mouth-watering, gluten free dishes that are simple and easy to prepare, thanks to the wonderful features of a slow cooker.

Gluten free eating has become a priority among today's health-conscious members of society. With the current rise in the number of people acquiring celiac disease, cancer, irritable bowel syndrome, food allergies and other health problems, medical research has determined that wheat products play a major part in this unhealthy cycle of illness. This discovery has led doctors and nutrition experts to encourage people to adopt a gluten free lifestyle wherein healthier, organic meals without wheat products should be consumed to achieve balance within the mind, body and spirit.

To help us achieve more balance in our health, this book provides gluten free recipes that we can incorporate in our daily meal preparation. The ingredients used in each dish are 100% gluten free and is cooked to perfection with the use of a slow cooker. We will also see how interesting gluten free cooking can be with the colorful mix of fruits, vegetables, dairy and meats found in each slow cooker meal. The dishes are easy to make and tasty that you might just get hooked on using the slow cooker every day.

Let's begin the journey.

Chapter 1: The Science behind a Gluten Free Diet

"It's bizarre that the produce manager is more important to my children's health then the pediatrician."

Meryl Streep

Over 20 million people across the world have adopted a zero-gluten lifestyle and have drastically changed the way they eat. Health food advocates have strongly claimed that eliminating wheat and other gluten-enriched products from their diet have helped them achieve a healthier body, clearer mind and a happier soul.

Let us find out the science behind this controversial protein and how it affects the balance within the human body:

The Composition of Gluten

Gluten in its simplest form is a protein found in food products made with wheat, barley, rye and other grain varieties. It is composed of two proteins: glutenin and gliadin. The reason why gluten grains are used in food preparation is due to its chemical composition that provides food with elasticity, thus making it softer and easier to chew.

It has been proven that bread has a high gluten content compared to most foods because the kneading process extracts more gluten strands and creates links with other proteins. However, processed food and artificial flavor enhancers have likewise been found to contain gluten, apart from other chemicals that are harmful to the body.

How Is Gluten Harmful to the Body?

A high consumption of gluten-enriched foods creates a negative autoimmune reaction within the body, hence making an individual more prone to allergies, illness and disorders. This response can be attributed to the body's reaction to gliadin, a sub-protein of gluten that creates abnormal activities within the digestive tract.

Once gluten enters the body and sticks to the digestive wall, the immune system treats it as a harmful element that needs to be eliminated. Automatically, the immune system attacks the gluten and in the process, damages the healthy cells of the stomach. The damaged cells of the intestines become the entry point for bacteria and other harmful chemicals into the body.

Some diseases that have been linked to regular gluten intake include celiac disease, irritable bowel syndrome, leaky gut syndrome, anemia, fatigue, food allergies and brain damage. Though celiac disease is known to be a genetically-inherited disease, other illnesses have developed due to gluten intolerance caused by eating huge portions of grain products.

The Benefits of a Gluten Free Diet

People who have taken the turn for the better and eliminated gluten from their diet have experienced the wonders of clean, healthy eating. Removing wheat products from one's diet and replacing it with fruits, vegetables, dairy and lean meats will help cleanse the system and protect the cells from degeneration.

Here are some of the health benefits of a gluten free diet:

- easier weight management

- less cravings for unhealthy food

- food allergies are eliminated

- treatment of celiac disease and other autoimmune diseases

- reduced IBS symptoms

- lesser risk of having stomach problems

- lower cholesterol and blood sugar levels

- reduced risk of heart disease and cancer

- have more energy for weight loss activities

- happier disposition

- brain disorder symptoms for people with autism, epilepsy and schizophrenia are easier to manage

Gluten Free Food Checklist

Before starting on your journey towards a healthier gluten free lifestyle, it is important to know which foods should be a part of your ingredient list and which ones should be eliminated from the pantry. Here is a list of foods to guide you in preparing healthier meals:

Safe Gluten Free Foods

- Gluten free flours and grains such as almond flour, millet, amaranth, buckwheat, sorghum, corn flour, cornmeal, potato flour, quinoa, rice (brown, white), teff flour, gluten free oats

- Fresh fruits, vegetables and herbs

- Beans, legumes and soy

- Healthy nuts and seeds

- Canned fruits, vegetables and juices, provided they do not contain artificial sweeteners or additives

- Dairy products such as butter, milk, eggs, cream, real cheese, gluten free yoghurt

- Red meat, chicken and seafood, provided that they are not breaded nor soaked in gluten-enriched marinades

- Healthy oils such as olive oil, coconut oil, sesame oil, canola oil

- Sweeteners such as sugar, honey, maple syrup, coconut sugar, agave

- Spices and seasonings such as vinegar, gluten free soy sauce, coconut aminos, ground spices, dried herbs

- Alcoholic beverages

- Baking products such as powdered pectin, xantham and guar gums, tapioca, baking powder, baking soda, vanilla

Gluten Products to Avoid

- Wheat-enriched recipes made with wheat flour, couscous, semolina, kamut, spelt, durum, triticale, modified wheat starch, cake flour

- Malt products such as malt vinegar, malt syrup, malt flavoring

- Barley products such as licorice, mock seafood meat, beer

- Artificial seasonings, sauces and marinades

- Rye

- Processed cheeses and cheese spreads

- Breads and pastries such as cakes, doughnuts, muffins, pretzels

In order to create a healthier kitchen, always check the grocery for gluten free alternatives of your favorite food. Otherwise, it is always best to stick to using organic, wheat-free ingredients when preparing meals for you and the whole family.

Transitioning to a gluten free lifestyle may seem challenging at first, but its benefits are worth every simple change that you are willing to make to your daily eating habits. Dining healthy and gluten free will help you achieve total wellness and a better life ahead.

Gluten free dishes can be prepared in a number of ways: grilling, frying, baking or steaming. However, an easier way to cook these delicious recipes is by using a slow cooker. You get the same flavor and nutrition without the hassle of spending countless hours in the kitchen.

The succeeding chapter will discuss the benefits of having a slow cooker in your gluten free kitchen and a few tips on how it can help novice chefs prepare nutritious and tasty meals.

Chapter 2: Slow Cooker Tips for Gluten Free Dishes

If you are a greenhorn at the kitchen, chances are you already feel intimidated by the thought of cutting, dicing, frying, baking, boiling and plating dishes for a lengthy amount of time. Let's face it: cooking delicious and gluten free treats does require a lot of time and energy.

However, there is a way to unburden your culinary anxiety, and that is by using a reliable and efficient slow cooker. It will simplify the cooking process and allow you to relax and enjoy your time while a delicious home-cooked meal is being prepared.

A slow cooker is every beginner chef's dream machine. Apart from it costing cheaper than an oven or outside grill, creating meals in a slow cooker is quick and easy. Just prepare the ingredients, place them all inside the pot, cover it, set the time and temperature then wait for the dish to cook. After a few hours, your gluten free recipe will turn out as appetizing as any other stove-top meal could be.

On the other hand, there is a huge difference between slow-cooking your ingredients and cooking great slow cooker dishes. Here are 6 basic tips that will help you create mouth-watering gluten free food while utilizing the incredible features of a slow cooker:

- Consider the right size slow cooker for your kitchen needs

If you are planning on purchasing a slow cooker, think of the volume of cooking that you usually do. If you have a small family of four, a 5-quart slow cooker would suit your kitchen. On the other hand, if you live solo and want to cook simple, gluten free meals while you are away at work, a smaller 3 ½ quart slow cooker will do.

The right size pot will enable you to cook ingredients properly without spilling over once the dish starts to simmer.

- Determine the most suitable cooking time and temperature

The slow cooker recipes in this e-book are flexible in terms of cooking time and can be set on either low or high temperatures. However, it would be best to determine the most suitable range for each dish as this would affect its quality and flavor.

Here is a basic measure of temperature and cooking time if you choose to prepare food in a slow cooker:

- If the recipe calls for a cooking time of less than 30 minutes, slow cook the dish on high heat for 2 hours or cook it on low heat for 6 hours;

- If the recipe calls for a cooking time of 30 minutes to an hour, slow cook the dish on high heat for 3 hours or cook it on low heat for 7 hours;

- If the recipe calls for a cooking time of 1-2 hours, slow cook the dish on high heat for 4 hours or cook it on low heat for 8 hours; and

- If the recipe calls for a cooking time of 2-4 hours, slow cook the dish on high heat for 5 hours or cook it on low heat for 9 hours.

For example, if you are preparing for dinner in the late afternoon, it is suggested that you cook your dish on high heat so that the process is quicker and the meal will be done in 3-4 hours.

On the other hand, it is advisable to cook gluten free dishes on low heat if you have enough time. This method may add another 3 hours of cooking but the lengthy simmering of ingredients will bring out the flavors of the dish.

- Keep the pot covered

Once you have set the time and the temperature of the slow cooker, cover it and leave it as it is unless the recipe requires you to mix the dish often. Frequent uncovering of the lid will release the heat inside the pot and affect the quality of your dish. This will likewise lead to adjustments in the timer and dishes take longer to cook than expected.

- Prepare your dishes in advance

Slow cookers are great kitchen appliances that will help you prepare flavorful meals for the family. In this light, it does help that a little planning and preparation is involved so that you can leave your slow cooker in the morning and allow the dish to be cooked while you are doing your daily activities.

Plan your slow cooker meals the night before. Slice and prepare the ingredients, place them in containers and chill them overnight. In the morning, mix all your ingredients in the slow cooker and leave it there to cook for hours. Experience the wonders of cooking without being stuck inside the kitchen.

- Brown your meat and onions for a little extra flavor

An extra tip to make gluten free meals more flavorful: if you have extra time on your hands, brown your onions and meat in a skillet before cooking it in a slow cooker. When you sauté your ingredients beforehand, the meat and onions caramelize and a savory glaze sticks to it. This adds a bit of sweetness and smokiness to the dish.

- Be experimental when preparing dishes in a slow cooker

This e-book contains 40 gluten free recipes that can be prepared with the ease of a slow cooker. Use the slow cooker to prepare breakfast, sauces, main entrées and even desserts: the possibilities are limitless. Be creative while cooking gluten free recipes. You will subsequently realize that owning a slow cooker gives you the freedom to enjoy quality time while concocting healthy and scrumptious meals for the whole family.

Gluten free dishes will be taste much better with these basic slow cooker tips. Try them out for yourself and make slow cooking a part of your healthy daily habits.

Chapter 3: Delicious and Gluten Free Breakfast Recipes

Slow Cooker Potato and Sausage Casserole

Preparation time: 30 minutes

Cooking time: 5 hours

Number of servings: 4

Ingredients:

- 1 ½ cups shredded potatoes
- 6 eggs, beaten
- 1 cup lean ground sausage
- ½ cup shredded Parmesan cheese
- 2 garlic cloves, minced
- ½ yellow onion, sliced
- ¼ cup fresh milk
- ½ tablespoon Dijon mustard
- Pinch of salt and pepper

Directions:

- Lightly grease the inside of the slow cooker with oil spray. Lay down the shredded potatoes inside the pot.

- In a small bowl, mix together the beaten eggs, milk, mustard, salt and pepper. Set this aside.

- Place a frying pan over medium high heat and sauté the garlic, onions and sausage. Once the sausage has turned golden brown, remove it from the heat and drain the excess oil. Place the browned sausage meat mixture on top of the grated potatoes.

- Sprinkle the grated cheese on top of the sausage meat. Slowly pour in the egg mixture over the sausage and potato layers and mix them together so that the ingredients are evenly distributed.

- Cover the pot and adjust the temperature to high. Cook the casserole for 5 hours until the casserole is firm to the touch.

- Place the casserole in a serving plate and enjoy!

Cinnamon Apple Oatmeal

Preparation time: 15 minutes

Cooking Time: 7 hours

Number of servings: 2

Ingredients:

- 2 cups peeled and chopped red apples

- 2 cups gluten free oatmeal

- 1 teaspoon cinnamon powder

- 2 tablespoons coconut oil

- ½ cup coconut sugar

- ½ cup fresh milk

Directions:

- Place the chopped apples in a slow cooker.

- Add the cinnamon powder, coconut oil and coconut sugar to the apples and mix well.

- Cover the pot and set the temperature to low. Slow-cook the oatmeal overnight for at least 7 hours.

- Spoon the oatmeal into individual bowls and drizzle some milk on top before serving.

Breakfast Rice Pudding

Preparation time: 5 minutes

Cooking time: 2 hours

Number of servings: 4

Ingredients:

- ¾ cup short grain white rice

- 1 cup water

- 1 ½ cup evaporated milk

- ½ cup honey

- ½ cup golden raisins

- ½ teaspoon cinnamon

- ½ teaspoon vanilla

- ½ teaspoon salt

Directions:

- Place the rice, water milk, honey, raisins, cinnamon, vanilla and salt in a slow cooker and mix well.

- Cover the slow cooker and set the temperature to high. Cook the pudding for 2 hours and stir every 30 minutes.

- Divide the pudding into individual bowls and serve it warm.

Slow Cooker Apple Spread on Toast

Preparation time: 15 minutes

Cooking time: 9 hours

Number of servings: 8

Ingredients:

- 12 Fuji apples, peeled and cored

- 2 teaspoons cinnamon powder

- 2 cups coconut sugar

- ¼ teaspoon salt

- ¼ teaspoon cloves

- 8 slices gluten-free bread, toasted

Directions:

- Chop the apples and place them in a slow cooker.

- Add in the cinnamon powder, coconut sugar, salt and cloves to the pot and mix well.

- Cover the slow cooker and set the temperature to high. Cook the apples for an hour but stir the mixture every 15 minutes.

- After an hour, adjust the slow cooker temperature to low and continue cooking the apple spread for 8 more hours.

- Once the apple spread is done, remove the lid and let it cool down to room temperature. Pour the spread into a bowl or jar then serve the apple spread with toasted gluten free bread for breakfast.

Cheese and Spinach Frittata

Preparation time: 10 minutes

Cooking time: 1 hour 30 minutes

Number of servings: 4

Ingredients:

- 1 ½ cups chopped spinach leaves
- 1 cup cottage cheese
- ½ cup chopped yellow onion
- 1 tomato, diced
- 3 tablespoons fresh milk
- 2 eggs
- 2 egg whites
- Salt and pepper to taste

Directions:

- Lightly brown the onions on a skillet and set this aside.
- Whisk the eggs and egg whites in a bowl. Add in the spinach, cheese, tomato, fresh milk, salt and pepper and mix well.

- Pour the frittata mixture into a slow cooker, cover it and set the temperature to low.

- Cook the frittata for 1 ½ hours until the eggs have been fully cooked.

- Transfer the frittata to a plate before serving.

Banana Quinoa Cereal

Preparation time: 10 minutes

Cooking time: 5 hours

Number of servings: 6

Ingredients:

- 1 ½ cups quinoa

- 2 bananas, mashed

- 4 tablespoons honey

- 1 tablespoon light cream

- 1 cup fresh milk

- 1 cup water

- ½ teaspoon vanilla extract

- 2 tablespoons melted butter

- 2 tablespoons chopped almonds

- Banana slices

Directions:

- Mix the honey and almonds in a bowl and blend well.

- Place the quinoa, light cream, fresh milk, water, vanilla and melted butter in a slow cooker. Add in the mashed bananas and the honey and nut mixture. Mix the ingredients well.

- Cover the pot and cook the cereal on low for 5 hours.

- Once the cereal is done, mix it with a wooden spoon and pour it into a serving bowl. Place a few slices of banana on top to garnish the cereal.

Slow Cooker Hard-boiled Eggs

Preparation time: 5 minutes

Cooking time: 8 hours

Number of servings: 8

Ingredients:

- 8 medium eggs

- 3 cups water

- 1 tablespoon olive oil

- 2 tablespoons ground coffee

Directions:

- Place the eggs, olive oil and ground coffee in a slow cooker.

- Set the temperature to the lowest range and cover the pot. Simmer the eggs for 8 hours.

- Peel the hard-boiled eggs before serving.

Homemade Strawberry Jam

Preparation time: 20 minutes

Cooking time: 4 hours

Number of servings: 5

Ingredients:

- 8 cups fresh strawberries, rinsed and hulled

- 3 cups granulated sugar

- 3 tablespoons fresh orange juice

- 4 tablespoons powdered pectin

Directions:

- Place the strawberries in a large bowl and crush them with a potato masher or a hand blender. Once the berries are crushed, place them in a slow cooker.

- Add the orange juice and powdered pectin to the crushed berries. Let it stand for 5-10 minutes.

- Pour the sugar into the slow cooker and mix well. Cover the pot and set the temperature to low. Cook the berries for 2 hours while stirring every 30 minutes.

- After 2 hours, remove the cover of the slow cooker and adjust the temperature to high. Cook the jam for another 2 hours.

- Pour the jam into heat resistant jars and let them cool down. Spread the jam onto your favorite morning pancakes or waffles.

Chapter 4: Non-Gluten Soups and Stews Slow-Cooked to Perfection

Hearty Tomato Soup

Preparation time: 15 minutes

Cooking time: 6 hours

Number of servings: 6

Ingredients:

- 4 cups diced fresh tomatoes

- 4 cups natural chicken stock

- 2 celery stalks, diced

- 1 tablespoon chopped basil

- 2 carrots, peeled and diced

- 1 onion, chopped

- 1 cup heavy cream

- 2 teaspoons sea salt

- ½ cup grated Parmesan cheese

Directions:

- Place the tomatoes, chicken broth, celery, carrots and onion inside the slow cooker. Cover the pot and cook the tomato mixture for 5 hours on high temperature.

- Once the vegetables are tender, pour the contents of the slow cooker into a blender but do pass it through a strainer. Discard the remaining solids and puree the tomato mixture until it becomes smooth.

- Pour the pureed tomato mixture back into the slow cooker then mix in the cream, salt and basil. Cover the pot and cook the soup for another hour.

- Once the soup is ready, pour it into a serving bowl and top it with the grated Parmesan cheese.

Chicken Soup for the Gluten-free Soul

Preparation time: 20 minutes

Cooking time: 5 hours

Number of servings: 4

Ingredients:

- 4 chicken breasts, rinsed and dried

- 7 garlic cloves, minced

- 1 tablespoon olive oil

- 8 baby potatoes, sliced

- 2 zucchinis, peeled and diced

- 1 yellow bell pepper, deseeded and diced

- 1 yellow summer squash, peeled and diced

- 2 cups shredded cabbage

- 2 medium tomatoes, diced

- 1 teaspoon oregano

- 1 teaspoon dried basil

- 1 teaspoon chopped fresh parsley

- 3 cups natural chicken broth

- 1 teaspoon balsamic vinegar

- ½ teaspoon honey

- Salt and pepper to taste

Directions:

- Drizzle the olive oil inside the crock pot then place the chicken breasts inside. Sprinkle some salt, pepper and the minced garlic on top of the chicken. Set this aside.

- In a separate bowl, mix together the potatoes, zucchinis, tomatoes, bell pepper, summer squash, cabbage, oregano, basil and parsley. Toss the vegetables with the spices then add in the balsamic vinegar, honey and a sprinkle of salt and pepper.

- Pour the mixed vegetables on top of the chicken breasts then add in the chicken broth.

- Cover the pot then place the temperature on high. Cook the soup for 5 hours or until the chicken is very tender.

Spicy Eggplant Stew

Preparation time: 15 minutes

Cooking time: 8 hours

Number of servings: 8

Ingredients:

- ½ cup fresh vegetable stock
- 1 ½ cup pureed tomatoes
- 2 garlic cloves, minced
- 2 ½ cups diced eggplant
- 1 cup chopped red onion
- 1 ½ cups diced zucchini
- 1 large tomato, chopped
- 1 ½ cups diced butternut squash
- 1 medium carrot, peeled and julienned
- 3 pieces frozen okra
- ¼ teaspoon paprika
- ¼ teaspoon chili powder
- ½ teaspoon cumin powder

- ½ teaspoon turmeric powder

- ½ teaspoon ground black pepper

- ½ teaspoon salt

Directions:

- Place the vegetable stock and pureed tomatoes inside the slow cooker. Add in the eggplant, garlic, onion, zucchini, tomato, butternut squash, carrot and okra and mix.

- Add in all the spices into the stew and mix well. Cover the pot and set the temperature to low. Cook the stew for 8 hours or until the vegetables are soft. Pour the eggplant stew into a large soup bowl before serving.

Slow-cooked Chili con Carne

Preparation time: 15 minutes

Cooking time: 6 hours

Number of servings: 6

Ingredients:

- 450 grams ground beef

- 1 cup beef stock

- 1 teaspoon chili powder

- 1 teaspoon paprika

- 2 teaspoons cinnamon powder

- 1 red bell pepper, deseeded and diced

- 2 cups diced tomatoes

- 1 yellow onion, chopped

- 2 garlic cloves, minced

- 2 cups pureed pumpkin

- 1 cup diced green chilies

Directions:

- Place the ground beef in the slow cooker and set the temperature to low.

- Add in the beef stock, chili powder, paprika and cinnamon powder into the slow cooker and mix. Stir in the bell pepper, tomatoes, onion, garlic, pureed pumpkin and green chilies.

- Cover the pot and cook the chili for 6 hours.

The Ultimate Sweet Potato Soup

Preparation time: 15 minutes

Cooking time: 8 hours

Number of servings: 8

Ingredients:

- 3 sweet potatoes, peeled and diced

- 1 cup chopped green beans

- 2 cups freshly-chopped tomatoes

- 1 yellow onion, chopped

- 3 celery stalks, chopped

- 1 ½ cup green lentils

- 4 carrots, chopped

- 5 garlic cloves, minced

- 8 cups natural broth (vegetable or chicken)

- 1 teaspoon dried oregano

- 1 teaspoon fresh rosemary

- Salt and pepper to taste

Directions:

- Set the temperature of the slow cooker to low.

- Add the sweet potatoes, green beans, tomatoes, onion, celery, lentils, carrots and garlic cloves into the slow cooker. Pour in the broth then sprinkle the oregano, rosemary, salt and pepper.

- Cover the pot and cook the sweet potato soup for 8 hours. Add a little more broth in the end if the soup seems too thick.

Quinoa and Beans Stew

Preparation time: 20 minutes

Cooking time: 5 hours

Number of servings: 8

Ingredients:

- 450 grams dried black beans, rinsed
- 1 cup raw quinoa, rinsed
- 6 cups water
- 2 dried red chilies
- 3 ½ cups chopped tomatoes
- 3 garlic cloves, minced
- 1 red onion, chopped
- 2 green bell peppers, deseeded and chopped
- ½ cup chopped fresh cilantro
- 1 teaspoon coriander powder
- 2 ½ teaspoons chili powder
- 1 teaspoon cinnamon powder
- Salt and pepper to taste

- Handful of chopped green onions

Directions:

- Place the black beans and quinoa into the slow cooker. Add in the water, chilies, tomatoes, garlic, onion, bell peppers and cilantro and stir.

- Sprinkle the coriander, chili and cinnamon powders on top of the stew. Finally, season it with salt and pepper.

- Cover the slow cooker and cook the stew on high for 5 hours. Sprinkle the chopped green onions on top before serving.

Slow Cooker Squash Soup

Preparation time: 15 minutes

Cooking time: 4 hours

Number of servings: 4

Ingredients:

- 2 cups chicken broth

- 1 cup fresh milk

- 2 cups chopped squash

- 2 teaspoons chopped cilantro

- 2 celery stalks, chopped

- ½ cup chopped carrots

- ¼ teaspoon salt

- ¼ teaspoon ground black pepper

- ½ cup grated Parmesan cheese

Directions:

- Place the chicken broth, squash, celery, carrots, salt and pepper in a slow cooker and mix them well. Cover the pot and set the temperature to high. Cook the soup for 4 hours until the vegetables are very soft.

- Uncover the pot and pour in the fresh milk. Mix the soup before pouring it in a serving bowl.

- Sprinkle the cilantro and cheese on top of the soup before serving.

Warm and Chunky Corn Chowder

Preparation time: 10 minutes

Cooking time: 6 hours

Number of servings: 4

Ingredients:

- 8 cups natural chicken broth

- 2 cups fresh or frozen corn kernels

- 1 carrot, peeled and chopped

- 1 large potato, chopped

- 1 red onion, chopped

- 1 red bell pepper, deseeded and chopped

- 1 tablespoon olive oil

Directions:

- Heat the olive oil in a pan and lightly sauté the onions.

- Once the onions have slightly browned, place them inside the slow cooker and add in the corn, potato, carrot, onion and bell pepper. Mix them well.

- Cover the slow cooker and set the temperature to high. Slow cook the chowder for 6 hours then turn it off.

- Pour the chowder into a blender and pulse for 2-3 times, making sure to leave some vegetable chunks in the chowder. Place the mixture in soup bowls before serving.

Chapter 5: Delightfully Simple Gluten Free Main Dishes

Slow-cooked Sweet Ham

Preparation time: 5 minutes

Cooking time: 6 hours 30 minutes

Number of servings: 8

Ingredients:

- 3 kg bone-in ham, unwrapped

- 3 cups pineapple juice

- 1 cup maple syrup

- ½ cup brown sugar

Directions:

- Place the ham in a large slow cooker. Rub the brown sugar on all sides of the meat.

- Pour the pineapple juice and maple syrup on top of the ham.

- Cover the pot and set the temperature to low. Cook for 7 hours or until the ham is tender once a fork is poked into it.

- Turn off the slow cooker and let the ham stand for 20 minutes.

- Remove the ham from the slow cooker and place it on a cutting board. Cut a few slices of the ham and place it on a serving dish together with the whole meat. Pour the sauce over the meat before serving.

Spicy Honey Sesame Chicken

Preparation time: 10 minutes

Cooking time: 4 hours

Number of servings: 6

Ingredients:

- 1 pound boneless and skinless chicken breasts
- 1 tablespoon chili powder
- 3 tablespoons raw honey
- 2 teaspoons sesame oil
- 2 tablespoons pureed tomatoes
- 1 teaspoon chopped chilies
- 1 teaspoon sesame seeds
- 1 teaspoon chopped green onions
- ½ cup chopped yellow onion
- 2 tablespoons apple cider vinegar
- 3 tablespoons gluten-free soy sauce
- 2 tablespoons water
- 1 teaspoon minced garlic

- 2 teaspoons corn starch

Directions:

- Dissolve the corn starch in water until it is free of lumps. Set this aside.

- In a separate bowl, mix together the soy sauce, apple cider vinegar, sesame oil, honey, chili powder and pureed tomatoes. Add in the yellow onions, garlic, chilies and chicken breasts and mix well.

- Place the chicken breasts inside the slow cooker and pour the sauce on top. Cover the slow cooker and set the temperature to high. Cook for 4 hours or until the chicken is tender.

- Top with green onions and sesame seeds before serving.

Slow-cooked Cabbage Rolls with Quinoa

Preparation time: 15 minutes

Cooking time: 6 hours

Number of servings: 8

Ingredients:

- 450 grams lean ground beef

- 8 cabbage leaves, boiled and drained

- ½ cup raw quinoa, washed and drained

- ¼ cup soy milk

- 2 garlic cloves, minced

- 1 red onion, minced

- 1 egg, beaten

- ¼ teaspoon ground black pepper

- ½ teaspoon salt

- 2 teaspoons gluten-free soy sauce

- 2 tablespoons coconut sugar

- 2 tablespoons apple cider vinegar

- 2 cups chopped tomatoes

Directions:

- In a small bowl, combine the chopped tomatoes, apple cider vinegar, coconut sugar and soy sauce. Mix well and set aside.

- On another bowl, mix together the ground beef, quinoa, soy milk, garlic, onion, egg, salt and pepper. Spoon a quarter cup of the beef mixture on the middle of a cabbage leaf, fold the sides over and roll it away from you. Do the same procedure for the rest of the cabbage leaves.

- Place the cabbage rolls inside the slow cooker. Pour the tomato mixture inside the pot and cover it.

- Set the temperature to low and cook the cabbage rolls for 6 hours. Place the rolls on a serving dish and pour the sauce over it before serving.

Lamb Curry with White Rice

Preparation time: 15 minutes

Cooking time: 3 hours

Number of servings: 3

Ingredients:

- 450 grams lamb shoulder

- 2 cups cooked white rice

- 1 ½ cup coconut milk

- 3 garlic cloves, minced

- 1 yellow onion, chopped

- 1 ½ tablespoons chopped ginger

- 2 tablespoons apple cider vinegar

- 1 teaspoon curry powder

- ¼ teaspoon turmeric powder

- ½ teaspoon mustard seeds

- ½ teaspoon ground coriander

- 1 teaspoon ground cumin

- ¼ teaspoon cinnamon powder

- ¼ teaspoon cayenne pepper

- 1 teaspoon salt

- ½ teaspoon ground black pepper

- ½ cup chopped fresh cilantro

Directions:

- Prepare the lamb by cutting it at the bone. Set this aside.

- Pour the coconut milk into the slow cooker. Add in the garlic, onion, ginger and vinegar and mix well.

- Mix the curry powder, turmeric, mustard seeds, coriander, cumin, cinnamon, cayenne, salt and pepper into the coconut milk mixture.

- Place the lamb pieces into the coconut milk and spices and mix well.

- Cover the slow cooker and set the temperature on high. Cook the lamb curry for 3 hours, until the meat separates from the bone.

- Once the meat is cooked, remove the bone pieces and discard.

- Place the cooked white rice on a serving dish. Spoon the lamb curry and place it on top of the rice, and sprinkle fresh cilantro on top before serving.

Creamy Beef Stroganoff

Preparation time: 15 minutes

Cooking time: 4 hours

Number of servings: 6

Ingredients:

- 900 grams lean ground beef

- 1 tablespoon olive oil

- 2 cups button mushrooms, halved

- 2 yellow onions, chopped

- 1 tablespoon minced garlic

- 1 cup coconut milk

- 1 cup plain yoghurt

- 1 cup natural beef stock

- 2 tablespoons gluten free soy sauce

- 2 tablespoons non-gluten mustard

- Pinch of salt and pepper

Directions:

- Heat the olive oil in a large skillet over medium heat. Fry the ground beef until it becomes slightly brown. Sprinkle some salt and pepper to taste. Once the beef is cooked, place it inside a large slow cooker.

- Add the mushrooms, onions, garlic, mustard and soy sauce to the ground beef and mix well. Lastly, pour in the coconut milk and beef stock and cover the slow cooker.

- Set the temperature to high and slow cook the beef for 3 ½ hours. Once the beef is cooked, pour it into a serving bowl and let it stand for 30 minutes. Spoon the yoghurt into the stroganoff and mix well before serving.

Gluten Free Vegan Gumbo

Preparation time: 20 minutes

Cooking time: 8 hours

Number of servings: 6 servings

Ingredients:

- 1 cup sliced okra

- 1 cup button mushrooms, halved

- 1 red onion, chopped

- 2 celery stalks, chopped

- 1 yellow bell pepper, deseeded and chopped

- 1 zucchini, sliced into quarters

- 1 eggplant, diced

- 3 garlic cloves, chopped

- 2 cups chopped tomatoes

- 2 cups canned kidney beans, washed and drained

- 2 cups water

- 3 tablespoons olive oil

- 2 tablespoons gluten free flour

- 2 tablespoons coconut aminos or non-gluten soy sauce

- 1 tablespoon chili powder

- ½ tablespoon cayenne pepper

- ½ tablespoon salt

- ½ tablespoon ground black pepper

- 3 cups cooked white rice

Directions:

- In a large skillet over medium flame, heat a tablespoon of the olive oil. Start sautéing the okra, mushrooms, onion, celery, bell pepper, zucchini and eggplant until slightly brown. Place the sautéed vegetables inside the slow cooker.

- On the same skillet, heat the remaining olive oil and add in the flour. Stir constantly while slowly pouring in the water. Allow the water to boil then pour it into the slow cooker.

- Add the tomatoes, kidney beans, coconut aminos, chili powder, cayenne powder, salt and pepper into the slow cooker. Mix all the ingredients and place a lid on the slow cooker.

- Adjust the cooker's temperature to low and cook the gumbo for 8 hours.

- Place the cooked rice on a serving platter. Pour the cooked gumbo on top of the rice and serve immediately.

Slow-cooked Herb Chicken

Preparation time: 15 minutes

Cooking time: 6 hours

Number of servings: 4

Ingredients:

- 7 garlic cloves, minced

- 1 yellow onion, chopped

- 1 carrot, peeled and chopped

- ½ teaspoon sea salt

- ½ teaspoon whole pepper

- 1 teaspoon sage

- 2 teaspoons rosemary

- 1 teaspoon thyme

- 1 whole chicken, neck and insides removed

- 3 cups cooked white rice or quinoa

Directions:

- Rinse the chicken with cold water and drain.

- Place the chopped onions and carrots inside the chicken and the chopped garlic in between the skin and the meat.

- In a small bowl, mix together the salt, pepper, sage, rosemary and thyme. Rub the spices onto the chicken.

- Place the chicken inside the slow cooker and adjust the temperature to high. Cover the pot and roast the chicken for 6 hours until the meat falls off the bone.

- Serve this dish with cooked rice or quinoa.

Slow Cooker Spicy Pork Chops

Preparation time: 20 minutes

Cooking time: 6 hours

Number of servings: 2

Ingredients:

- 4 pork chops

- 1 tablespoon gluten free soy sauce

- 1/3 cup water

- 1 tablespoon olive oil

- 1 cup gluten free ketchup (ex. Heinz)

- 1 teaspoon chili powder

- ½ cup chopped yellow onion

- 2 garlic cloves

- Pinch of salt and pepper

Directions:

- Place a skillet over medium heat and heat the olive oil. Add the onions to the pan and sauté until it turn light brown.

- Next, add in the garlic, ketchup, soy sauce, salt, pepper, chili powder and water. Allow the sauce to simmer for 8-10 minutes.

- Place the pork chops inside the slow cooker and pour the sauce over it. Cover the pot and cook the pork chops on low heat for 6 hours.

- Once the chops are cooked, place them on a serving dish and drizzle the sauce on top.

Chapter 6: Slow Cooker Dessert Recipes for the Sweet

Gluten Free Brownie Balls

Preparation time: 10 minutes

Cooking time: 3 hours

Number of servings: 8

Ingredients:

- 1 cup unsweetened cocoa powder

- 2 cups almond flour

- 2 eggs, beaten

- 1 cup coconut sugar

- ½ cup coconut milk

- ½ cup water

- ½ cup coconut oil

- 2 teaspoons baking soda

- 2 teaspoons baking powder

- 2 teaspoons vanilla

- 1 teaspoon salt

Directions:

- Drizzle the coconut oil in the slow cooker and spread it around the base.

- Place the flour, cocoa powder, sugar, baking powder, baking soda and salt into the pot and mix well.

- Pour the eggs, coconut milk, water and vanilla onto the dry ingredients and blend them together with a wooden spoon.

- Cover the pot and cook the brownie batter on low for 3 hours.

- After 3 hours, turn off the slow cooker and let the brownie batter cool for 30 minutes. Once it has cooled down, scoop tablespoonfuls of the mixture then use your hands to form them into balls. Place them on a nice dish and serve.

Slow-cooked Bananas Foster

Preparation time: 15 minutes

Cooking time: 2 hours

Number of servings: 5

Ingredients:

- 5 bananas, peeled and sliced

- 1 cup coconut sugar

- 4 tablespoons melted butter

- ½ cup chopped almonds

- ¼ cup rum

- ½ teaspoon cinnamon powder

- ½ cup grated coconut

Directions:

- In a small bowl, mix together the coconut sugar, butter, rum and cinnamon. Set this aside.

- Arrange the banana slices inside the slow cooker. Pour the sugar and rum mixture on top of the bananas and cover it.

- Cook the bananas on low heat for 2 hours. Sprinkle the coconut and almonds on top within the last 15 minutes of cooking.

- Serve this dessert by itself or with a scoop of vanilla ice cream.

Scrumptious Crème Brulee

Preparation time: 10 minutes

Cooking time: 4 hours

Number of servings: 4

Ingredients:

- 5 egg yolks

- ½ cup white sugar

- ¼ cup raw sugar

- 2 cups whipping cream

- 1 tablespoon vanilla

Directions:

- In a large bowl, whip the egg yolks while slowly adding the white sugar and whipping cream. Add in the vanilla and mix well.

- Place the crème brulee mixture in a baking dish that will fit inside the slow cooker. Set this aside.

- To create a water bath for the crème brulee, pour some water into the slow cooker. Place the baking dish with the crème brulee mixture inside of it while making sure that the water is halfway up the top of the baking dish.

- Cover the slow cooker. Set the temperature to high and cook the crème brulee for 4 hours.

- After 4 hours, turn off the slow cooker and remove the baking dish. Let the dessert cool for 30 minutes.

- Sprinkle the raw sugar on top then slightly brown it with a handy butane torch to create a crisp topping. Serve immediately.

Slow Cooker Caramelized Peaches

Preparation time: 20 minutes

Cooking time: 2 hours

Number of servings: 10

Ingredients:

- 10 peaches, peeled, pitted and sliced

- ½ cup butter

- 1 cup coconut sugar

- ½ teaspoon powdered cloves

- ½ teaspoon cinnamon powder

- Scoop of gluten free ice cream*

Directions:

- Place peaches, butter, coconut sugar, cloves and cinnamon in a slow cooker and mix.

- Set the temperature to low and cover the slow cooker. Leave the peaches to caramelize for 2 hours then turn off the heat.

- To arrange this dessert, divide the peaches into individual bowls and place a scoop of ice cream on top. Serve immediately.

- Gluten free ice cream variants are available among popular brands such as Haagen-Dazs, Edy's and Breyer's. Be sure to check the labels.

Banana Bread Pudding

Preparation time: 15 minutes

Cooking time: 2 hours

Number of servings: 5

Ingredients:

- 5 bananas, peeled and chopped
- 6 cups cubed gluten free bread
- ½ cup maple syrup
- ½ cup granulated sugar
- ½ cup toasted pecans
- Pinch of salt
- 1 teaspoon brandy or rum
- ½ teaspoon minced ginger
- ½ teaspoon cinnamon powder
- ½ teaspoon nutmeg
- ½ cup almond milk
- 1 teaspoon butter

Directions:

- In a mixing bowl, combine the sugar, pecans, brandy and bananas. Mix them well and set it aside.

- In a separate bowl, mix together the almond milk, maple syrup, ginger, cinnamon, nutmeg and salt. Pour in the cubed bread and coat it with the milk mixture. Set this aside as well.

- Lightly grease the bottom of the slow cooker with butter. Slowly pour in a half of the milk and bread mixture into the pot then spoon one half of the banana mixture on top of it. Repeat the same order of layering.

- Cover the pot and set the temperature to high. Cook the bread pudding for an hour and 45 minutes. Once the pudding is firm, turn off the slow cooker and serve it while it's hot.

Sliced Pears with Gooey Butterscotch Sauce

Preparation time: 10 minutes

Cooking time: 1 hour 10 minutes

Number of servings: 4

Ingredients:

- 2 apples, cored and sliced

- 2 ¾ cup butterscotch chips

- 1 tablespoon rum

- ½ cup evaporated milk

- ½ cup finely chopped almonds

Directions:

- Place the milk and butterscotch chips in a slow cooker, cover it and cook on low heat for 1 hour. Stir the butterscotch sauce every 15 minutes.

- After an hour, turn off the slow cooker. Add the rum and chopped almonds into the butterscotch and mix well. Pour the prepared butterscotch in a sauce bowl.

- Arrange the apple slices on the sides of a serving dish. Place the butterscotch sauce at the middle or dunk a few pieces of fruit into the sauce. Serve immediately.

Homemade Chocolate Fudge

Preparation time: 5 minutes

Cooking time: 8 hours 10 minutes

Number of servings: 5

Ingredients:

- ¼ cup coconut milk

- 2 ½ cup dark chocolate chips

- ¼ cup raw honey

- 1 teaspoon vanilla extract

- Pinch of sea salt

Directions:

- Place the milk, chocolate chips, honey, vanilla and salt in a slow cooker and mix well.

- Cover the pot and set the temperature to low. Cook the fudge for 2 hours but do not stir it.

- After 2 hours, turn off the slow cooker and uncover it. Lightly stir the fudge then leave it to cool for 3 hours.

- Once the fudge has reached room temperature, use a wooden spoon to beat it for 10 minutes. Pour the fudge into a greased dish, cover it with plastic wrap then place it in a freezer for 3 hours.

- Slice the chocolate fudge into squares before serving.

Slow Cooker Caramel Apples

Preparation time: 15 minutes

Cooking time: 1 hour

Number of servings: 6

Ingredients:

- 6 red apples, preferably Fuji or Gala variants

- 2 cups caramel candy cubes

- ¼ cup water

- Pinch of salt

- Popsicle sticks and wax paper

Directions:

- Wash the apples and remove the stems. Pierce a popsicle stick halfway through each of the apples. Set this aside.

- Place the caramel candies, salt and water inside a slow cooker. Cover it and cook the caramel on high for one hour.

- Turn off the slow cooker and uncover it. Dip each apple into the caramel sauce, let the excess drip and place it on a sheet of wax paper to cool.

Chapter 7: Savory Dips, Sauces and Side Dishes Prepared With a Slow Cooker

Slow-cooked Caramelized Onions

Preparation time: 15 minutes

Cooking time: 5 hours

Number of servings: 4

Ingredients:

- 6 white onions, chopped into thin slices

- 1 teaspoon salt

- 2 tablespoons olive oil

- 1 teaspoon sugar

Directions:

- Place the onions inside a slow cooker and add in the salt, sugar and olive oil.

- Cover the pot and set the temperature to low. Leave the onions to cook for 5 hours.

- Enjoy this sweet side dish with burgers, barbecued ribs or pulled pork sandwiches.

Gluten Free Marinara Sauce

Preparation time: 30 minutes

Cooking time: 10 hours

Number of servings: 15

Ingredients:

- 5 pounds chopped tomatoes
- 8 garlic cloves, chopped
- 3 onions, chopped
- ½ cup chopped fresh basil
- 1 cup chopped carrots
- ½ cup chopped fresh parsley
- ½ teaspoon cayenne pepper
- ½ cup olive oil
- 1 tablespoon sea salt

Directions:

- Place the tomatoes, garlic, onion and carrots in a slow cooker.

- Add in the basil, parsley, pepper, olive oil and sea salt and mix well.

- Cover the pot and set the temperature to low. Cook the sauce for 10 hours and use a hand blender to mash up the tomatoes inside the pot.

- Cool down the sauce and pour it into sterilized jars. Freeze the marinara sauce for a longer shelf life.

Spicy Tomato and Lentil Salsa

Preparation time: 10 minutes

Cooking time: 6 hours

Number of servings: 2

Ingredients:

- 1 ¾ cup chopped tomatoes

- ¼ cup green lentils

- ¼ cup gluten free salsa

- 3 garlic cloves, minced

- 1 red onion, chopped

- 2 teaspoons chili powder

- ¼ teaspoon ground cumin

- 1 teaspoon honey

Directions:

- Place the tomatoes, lentils, salsa, garlic, onion, chili powder, cumin and honey in a slow cooker and cover it with a lid.

- Set the temperature to low and cook the sauce for 6 hours.

- Serve this dip with gluten free chips or crackers.

Cheesy Artichoke Dip

Preparation time: 15 minutes

Cooking time: 1 hour

Number of servings: 4

Ingredients:

- 2 cups chopped artichoke hearts, rinsed and drained
- 1 cup chopped spinach
- ½ cup sour cream
- ½ cup plain yoghurt
- 5 garlic cloves, minced
- 2 cups shredded Parmesan cheese

Directions:

- Place the artichoke and spinach inside the slow cooker.
- Pour in the sour cream, yoghurt, cheese and garlic. Mix the ingredients together.
- Set the cooker's temperature to high and cook the dip for an hour.
- Pour the dip in a bowl and serve with sliced carrots, cucumbers or gluten free crackers.

Slow Cooker Cranberry Sauce

Preparation time: 10 minutes

Cooking time: 4 hours

Number of servings: 8

Ingredients:

- 900 grams fresh cranberries
- 450 grams red apples, peeled, cored and sliced
- 1 cup honey
- 4 teaspoons cinnamon powder
- ½ cup fresh orange juice

Directions:

- Place the apples, orange juice, cinnamon powder and cranberries in a slow cooker and cover it.
- Set the crock pot's temperature to high and cook the fruits for 4 hours.
- After 4 hours, allow the fruit mixture to cool then pour it into a blender. Puree the fruits completely then mix in the honey.
- Pour the sauce in a serving bowl or store it in the freezer inside mason jars

Healthy Mock Mashed Potatoes

Preparation time: 10 minutes

Cooking time: 5 hours

Number of servings: 4

Ingredients:

- 1 cup almond milk

- 2 cups water

- 1 cauliflower cut into florets

- 5 garlic cloves

- 1 bay leaf

- 1 tablespoon gluten free butter

- 1 teaspoon salt

Directions:

- Place the florets inside the slow cooker. Add in the salt, water, garlic cloves and bay leaf.

- Cover the pot and cook for 5 hours on low temperature.

- After 5 hours, remove the bay leaf and garlic cloves. Add in the butter and allow it to melt.

- Mash the cauliflower mixture with a hand blender or a potato masher. While mashing, slowly pour the milk to make the mixture creamier. The final product of this side dish should be similar to the texture of creamy mashed potatoes.

Slow Cooker Sausage Dip

Preparation time: 10 minutes

Cooking time: 25 minutes

Number of servings: 20

Ingredients:

- 600 grams spicy pork sausage, casing removed

- 1 ½ tablespoon olive oil

- 2 cups chopped tomatoes

- 1 tablespoon chopped green chilies

- 1 cup cream cheese

Directions:

- Heat the olive oil in a large skillet over medium heat. Add the pork sausage stuffing and sauté until golden brown. Drain the excess oil from the meat and place it inside the slow cooker.

- Add the cream cheese, tomatoes and green chilies into the sautéed sausage and cover the pot.

- Set the temperature to medium heat and cook the dip for 25 minutes while stirring constantly. Serve immediately.

Sweetened Cream of Corn

Preparation time: 10 minutes

Cooking time: 3 hours

Number of servings: 12 servings

Ingredients:

- 1 ½ cup cream cheese, cut into cubes

- 1 cup cottage cheese

- 6 cups frozen corn kernels

- ½ cup butter, cut into cubes

- 2 tablespoons honey

- 4 tablespoons milk

- 2 tablespoons water

Directions:

- Place the cream cheese, cottage cheese, corn, butter, honey, milk and water in a slow cooker and mix well.

- Cover the pot and set the temperature to low. Cook the corn mixture for 3 hours.

- Mix the creamed corn evenly before serving it as a side dish.

Conclusion

I hope this book was able to help you to cook gluten free dishes with confidence and ease with the use of a reliable and efficient slow cooker.

The next step is to try preparing healthier dishes on a daily basis that will not only satisfy the palate but also help you and the family become healthier and happier. Always remember that a gluten free lifestyle will help you achieve total wellness, and what better way to balance your body and energy than by enjoying a slow-cooked meal.

I wish you the best of luck!

To your success,

John Web